Fun B

By Liza Charlesworth

ISBN: 978-1-339-02664-0

Art Director: Tannaz Fassihi; Designer: Tanya Chernyak
Photos © Getty Images.
Copyright © Liza Charlesworth. All rights reserved. Published by Scholastic Inc.

3 4 5 6 7 8 9 10   68   32 31 30 29 28 27 26 25 24

Printed in Jiaxing, China. First printing, August 2023.

MSCHOLASTIC

It is a bug!
A bug is NOT big.

A bug has six legs.
1, 2, 3, 4, 5, 6!

A bug can run.
Run in the sun, bug!

Bugs can dig.
Dig in the mud, bug!

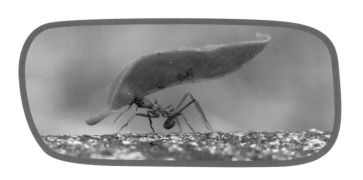

A bug can tug and lug.

It can flap up, up, up.

It can buzz on a bud.
Buzz, buzz!

A bug can sit on a pup.
A bug is fun!